Progressive Web Apps for Social Development

By Bishnu Goswami and Rohin Chatterjee

Progressive Web Apps for Social Development

By Bishnu Goswami
and
Rohin Chatterjee

This page intentionally kept blank

PREFACE

Our global landscape is one where technology is becoming a larger and larger fundamental part of everyday life. Technological landscapes are now merging with global landscapes and one may not find one without the other. Business and social interactions are also finding its way onto the technological landscapes. Due to the enormous reach of the instruments of the technological landscape, especially the mobile phone and fast internet, it is also a time when social development can be ushered through the use of the tools in this technological landscapes.

Progressive Web Apps are software applications which leverages on modern web capabilities to deliver an app-esque feel for users. These apps have advantages of being able to run in most mobile devices, while preserving the use of the latest technologies in web. Therefore, creating these apps, instead of more traditional desktop or mobile ones, can be very fitting in its role of social development.

In this book, we delve into the basics of using web apps for social development. Some use cases are highlighted for situations of civil unrests in fragile countries, and some use cases are highlighted for some growing problems of developed countries too. Then a short section introduces the reader on how to make a very simple Progressive Web App. Later in the book, some web apps which were previously designed with many of the core tenants of Progressive Web Apps are shown to the reader, and how these can create a positive change in many lives, discussed.

We hope the readers can feel the excitement of this new field as much as we do, and we also hope at least some of the readers to hop on this PWA train too!

Happy reading!

INTRODUCTION

The modern times is termed as the Age of Information. Perhaps no other term can replace this three-word-aggregate to best describe our modern life. The onset of this age was spearheaded by the digital revolution, which exerted perhaps the greatest revolution in humankind in centuries, neck-in-neck with the paradigm shifts such as the Renaissance and the discovery of planned agriculture.

The phenomenal growth of information and the ways we use it was unforeseen, even by many workers in this field. Advances in computing power, for example, now helps us to do mathematical calculations in minutes on our smartphones which took years in dedicated supercomputers, only a few decades ago. Unlike many modern innovations since the Industrial revolution, the information age has seen the users of all walks of life, ranging from land laborers in sub-Saharan Africa to billionaires in highly developed countries!

More interestingly, users in both the extremes often have access to technologies that differs so very little[1] that makes us wonder if there was anything more equal since the hunter-gatherer days of mankind.

We all know about the internet (this was niche information only 20 years ago!). But we often miss *how great* of an enabler it is, for almost all of the 7 billion people living in the world today. Encompassing every country (with some restrictions [2]) of the world, the internet rose above all the pettiness and narrow-minded oppression politics, giving mankind the liberty to both access information and egress information.

Every civilization has a currency. Every country has a currency. Our current age of information also has one, and that currency is information itself (majorly). The rosy side of this age is the fact that the currency of information is scattered throughout the world, away from locked out vaults (like Fort Knox with Gold). People willing to enter and flourish in the knowledge economy can do so with less restrictions than ever before. This is indeed one of the main reasons why developing countries are not poor but developing at a rapid pace. Some very highly developed countries see lesser growth (saturation), but the growth in developing countries such as India and China in recent decades has been *staggering*. This also does not come at the expense of the already developed nations, resulting in a win-win situation for all! Some populist notions try to discredit this fact but the bottom line of overall development in most countries stays steady as a rock!

Everything has its positives and negatives, especially for such big game changers like the digital revolution of this information age. The way forward in these situations is to first assert a contrarian non-binary stance! In social development initiatives, the focus on this book, we see this to be often violated. In the early days of the digital revolution (1960-70s) there was a wide backlash against the use of digital technologies, with the fear that it will cost many jobs. In the developing and newly industrialized countries, the backlash came over and over again, often in a very binary fashion. "No computers" was a popular slogan in many circles. Nowadays we will scoff at such a notion, because the technology involving computers is so much of an integral part in our lives. But simple scoffing is again binary, and we have to understand the valid reasons for such a fear and if it is still relevant today.

The benefits that this new age brings are pretty self-explanatory to any modern audience, so we are focusing more on the drawbacks.

The initial wave of digital technologies took away some jobs (stenographers, personal assistants in a model office; and manufacturing in case of the industries) but created many others too. Additionally, the process of outsourcing, which sometimes have a knee-jerk reaction against it by many populist leaders, is often an exercise in win-win. Developing countries have greatly improved their standards of living by this process of outsourcing alone, but it cannot be doubted that the growth in developed countries was still there, albeit somewhat slower due to the pre-saturation of the aforesaid standards.

The nitty-gritty of the previous paragraph shall not be discussed here as a bigger potential problem stays ahead of us. The digital technological revolution is entering a new wave, the wave of artificial intelligence, machine learning and better automation. This brings along a host of new exciting promises, but also some ominous signs, especially in relation to the job market.

DEMOCRACY AND DISTRIBUTION

Human beings are social animals. In a society, there is always a tug of war between the individual's wants and the wants of the other members, either singularly or as a whole. This is a cost which comes along with the benefits the society brings (let us go back to 1960s and say "This is a small step for a man..." to illustrate what a society as a whole can bring). To get the best out of this dichotomous situation, the concept of democracy got the most popularity and is the dominant form of government in most countries worldwide. In the absence of a proper democracy, the form of government which glues together any nation of respectable stature must have certain important qualities of 'in-practice' democracies nevertheless, such as looking after the welfare of its citizens, especially those who are downtrodden. Sometimes the looking after is inadequate, but in almost all the cases an attempt is exhibited, establishing the process as one which modern societies should adhere to.

Many manufacturing jobs were lost when many traditional industries took up automation. This has very early origins. Without getting into too much detail, we can touch upon two of these, in relatively modern times:

- The industrial revolution: Some countries of Europe got very rich and developed during this time due to the rise of manufacturing technologies. Millions of workers in handicrafts and traditional out-of-factory manufacturing lost their livelihood. Oppression of the British against India is one example to touch upon in this regard. Notable was the absence of aid which increased the suffering greatly.
- The automobile robotics revolution: This can be easily relatable to North American readers. The rise of robotics and global competition affected manufacturing jobs, where robots made the process more reliable, faster, scalable and very cost effective. But, many jobs were lost.

The take-home message here is the fact that in any important technological paradigm-shift, some job market disruption is to be expected. However, this also necessitates a proper understanding of the ways on how the negative aspects of a newly entering technology can be managed, and possibly used as an advantage in themselves.

In a proper democracy, no citizen should ideally be left out. Left out citizens can lower the immediate quality of life of the whole society (thievery, robbery and underground activities) in addition to the fact that the act of exclusion itself is myopic.

INFORMATIONAL CURRENCY MANAGEMENT FOR THE WEAKER SECTIONS OF THE SOCIETY

Our Moral Science teacher once told us a beautiful line; "It is easy to make a first boy (academically brilliant) first in class again (rankings), what is challenging is to make the weaker students better". I really liked this due to the following reasons:

- It spoke of a challenge. Easy things are a dime a dozen. Challenging things is what gives life a greater purpose and satisfies the Maslovian Self Actualization.
- It did not go to an overly simplistic rhetoric, which is impossible in practice. It did not say "Let's make the last boy first".
- It dazzles with hope!

Having established that in the information age, information itself is a major currency, we have to see what problems the weaker sections of the society face. After that we have to find how we can help them to manage their currency better.

Two of the major problems we are facing in this regard are:

- Fraud: From fiat money in modern economy, a parallel can be drawn. The middle class and upper class in most economies have their money managed by relatively reliable means. For example, the ultra wealthy have firms dedicated to the management of their assets. The middle class often invest in professionally managed mutual funds. However, the weaker sections often have no management of their funds or high-risk schemes such as the lottery, online gambling and Chit Funds (in India). This makes them susceptible to fraud. It is similar for the information-currency. Here, however, the economically weaker (in money terms) sections get affected more than the technology-deficient but economically stronger sections of the society. An example would be credit-card fraud against gullible tech users.

The credit card companies often have to adjust for the losses, but not the users themselves. But economically weaker sections (especially away from developed countries) often have little such padding in cases of fraud. Sometimes, various social schemes are made for the poorer sections of the society involving the information-currency, but a large portion of money gets swindled away. This is also a kind of fraud.

- Unwillingness to offer 'loans': Weaker sections of the society are often turned away from being offered monetary loans, and also 'loans' in a more general sense. Two main factors are at play here. One is the higher risk of defaulting by the weaker sections. The second is the oft-dominant populist practices of "waiving off loans", instead of their repayment by the government itself. In case of the more general sense, populist governments play the religion or race card and ignore the provision of 'loans' that could have benefited all. Few companies (or other organizations) are willing to build and maintain apps for the weaker sections of the society, in the absence of immediate profit pathways or hindrances in entering a market (the latter is usually becoming less of a problem though) . This is in contrast to the scenario observed in popular e-commerce sites of developing countries. In these sites where the middle class consumer culture dominates, the company often runs at losses for years. Yet these get the money flow in anticipation of future profits. This is not to say that shareholders should not care about money, but to say that loans for weaker sections of the societies can also fetch high returns, but in a larger timescale. This is a core tenet of proper inclusive development, and it serves to remind us that inclusive development is not just some "aids to the poor". The higher return is shown in the simple example of the development of tiger economies and countries like India, where the average income had trebled in the last few decades and a lot of profits have benefited the shareholders, both nationally and internationally, along with inclusive development being done , although somewhat inefficiently than what could have been.

With these problems in mind, the solutions can be sought which is well tuned with the information age. Many important questions can be raised in this regard. Here are a couple of them, with a focus on oft neglected implementation details:-

1) How can the weaker sections of the society make themselves a part of the modern economy, not just in spirit but in practice?
2) How can the weaker sections of the society get access to the choices of the modern economy, and not just only a handful of them deemed useful by the government?
3) How can the weaker sections learn to avoid fraud, which costs them the most compared to other better off sections of the society?

4) How can weaker sections of the society get included in the money flow of a good economy? In most cases, what happens in practice is that they get excluded from the real benefits by middle men and corrupt officials and themselves get made the scapegoat later.

5) How can one reliably understand the problems faced by the weaker sections (especially in developing countries, which this book is mostly focused at)? Media stories are often biased and extremely populist, which is an antithesis to statistics. How can we reduce guesstimates and get the real data?

It must also be understood that many basic services the middle and upper classes take for granted are often unavailable or inadequate for the weaker sections of the society. Public health, private health and emergencies are just a few of them.

While we will not cover all the aspects of Progressive Web Apps in this book, we will touch upon some prototypes pertaining to the last paragraph here. We will briefly explore in this book how PWAs can help and can usher a revolution in these fields, with a portion of the work already being started.

SITUATIONS OF CIVIL UNREST, WAR and EMERGENCIES.

In many areas of the world, there exists danger and an instability that is a threat to citizens worldwide. For example, in the Rwandan genocide of 1994, between the Hutus and Tutsis, more than a million people lost their lives . The destabilization from this violence has continued, and many hundreds of thousands of people are still in danger, either for their lives or for their livelihoods. This destabilization effect often spill over the borders to the whole continent and beyond. Marginalized groups such as the Tutsis in this case, may feel unsafe and in danger often. In the absence of direct intervention by the major powers of the world, which carries its own baggage and is often frowned upon, a relatively new kind of "force" (service) can restrict the effects of these slaughtering and war. This service is offered pretty much in all areas of the world. This would be cellular reception and the associated phone applications.

Phones are constantly connecting and exchanging information over these cellular networks. As the most basic example, the thing that could be sent over the network would be distress calls. If a progressive web app was made to cater to the needs of someone in need of prompt help, many more people could feel at ease. Given the maintenance required to keep up with updating and debugging Native Apps, Progressive Web Apps could be beneficial to people in need. All these are possible in a scenario when the cellular networks are kept operational, which is often the case before the real war starts, when these networks are sometimes turned off by the ruling governments.

To take the subject off a bit from the grim realities of the actual war, the movie Hotel Rwanda is a striking film that shows how the people were reacting to the chaos that ensued due to the violence. The Hotel that the main character chartered helped amid the mess, as many people were able to find safety in the midst of violence and instability. Many people were still in need, though. These people were afraid to seek help, as they were not sure about who they could trust. Isolated incidents similar to these could be something covered by Progressive Web Apps, as most people have access to a smartphones these days, even in the developing countries. Authorities could follow the signal of the person sending out a distress signal, and deliver the help required. This is vitally required in many parts of the developing world as the blueprint of establishments like hotels are often unavailable to emergency services in the absence of regularization. The film is based on an actual war between the Hutus and Tutsis.

Continuing with this civil-war example, these particular groups began to have tension after the Belgian colonization declared that Hutus were superior to the Tutsis. This started hatred stemming from ethnicity. The first instance of violence was in 1972, when the Tutsis targeted Hutus and killed between 80,000 to 200,000 citizens. The Hutus fought the Tutsis, and people opposing their governmental rule. The Rwandan genocide was when Hutus targeted Tutsis in 1994. In all, there was anywhere from 500,000 to 1,000,000 casualties resulting from the fighting. Technology could have paid a great deal in assuaging this amount of devastation. The Progressive Web Apps could help deliver help to people who are out of the way or unsure of the state of safety in the area. The violence was also in a way sponsored by state leaders, so having an app that would connect to reliable support would be beneficial for people, especially in this situation. Of course, this is a very simplified use-case of the technology. However, in situations where, say, the cellular networks were blocked, offline content can still provide information about safe havens. This is not available for traditional web-apps, but is available for Progressive Web Apps which supports offline content in its default use-case. Additionally, in the case when the network is not totally blocked, tools such as VPNs and the Tor network can also be used. A simple Progressive Web App can merely show that these options exist, as many people are unaware of these tools, often made specifically for these situations. A history about the Tor network can be interesting to the reader of this book in this regard.

A dissolving of factions existing in Rwanda would have lessened the impact of the violence as other people on the outside could have added to the situation amid the crisis. External power-projection, such as from countries like the U.S, need not be total military deployment, as political pressures are often enough to allay events such as possible civil-wars.

Cellular reception is also a technological innovation that is becoming increasingly more accessible to everyone, especially in countries which are showing a rapid growth rate. In 2018, the billionaire Mukesh Ambani spent 33 billion on Jio 4G Networks across India, increasing the strength and availability of the signal across the nation. This initiative increased the availability of connections and made it possible for more to connect to the world through the internet. Currently, the Jio signal is found 91.6% of the time in a random (populated) location nationally. This is a high number, meaning that many are able to share data and connect with others worldwide. People are able to harness the outreach and signal of these networks in order to create a means for distributing information over the Internet. Access to the internet through the use of mobile and handheld devices gives a dearth of information to people who may have difficulty accessing information in other means. If someone was in need of help on the go, a safety app with integration to the Progressive Web principles could be the help the person needed at that point in time.

SITUATIONS in PUBLIC HEALTH

Public health is often in the doldrums for many developing nations (and also in developed ones, for example the Opioid crisis in the USA). This state of affairs continues with a lot still to be done, despite sustained efforts and improvements over the years.

One of the dire situations in Public Health occurs in the realm of vector borne diseases. In 2015 alone, an estimated half a million people[3] died from Malaria alone. Other diseases, such as Dengue and Chikunguniya are also causing a lot of human suffering. There are obviously a set of different diseases and public health problems, but this example of vector borne diseases exemplifies what can be (rather) easily prevented.

In Public Health, one of the other important issue is the issue of effective communication. Government initiatives, often the sole way for weaker sections of the society for upliftment, are often needlessly bureaucratic. Therefore, the needs of the weaker sections are often met only partially, and often in an inefficient way.

Private players are rare in this field in absence of immediate profit roadmaps favored by them. Moreover, if the justice and regulative systems of a government is not in place properly, this can make things worse rather than better for the weaker sections of the society. Although there are some considerable social welfare efforts by some of the biggest companies in the world, the supply seems to be much less than the demands.

This leaves the field most accessible for small-scale NGOs and the departments of the government which can work rather independently without many bureaucratic hurdles. These factors also sync with the strengths our main topic in the book offers.

SITUATIONS in PUBLIC HEALTH: Opioid Crisis

One issue plaguing many countries worldwide and the United States in particular is the Opioid crisis. Related to this Opioid crisis is the problem with addictive drugs in general. This occurs when a user uses prescription pills, heroin, and synthetic pain relievers such as fentanyl for misuse and addiction. This creates instability in a nation as there are people who are depending on unnatural items in order to function and takes away from their productivity. There are many other ways in which a nation or a society gets affected negatively when these drugs are used by a non-negligible portion of the population. It also creates crises elsewhere as a group in power reaps the rewards of the drug trade. This leads to abuse of power, often even hurting groups of people in order to reach their goals of production. If people were instructed to be aware of the dangers of Opioids, in a fashion more apt with this age of technology, along-with the services provided by agencies such as the Drug Enforcement Administration (DEA) in the USA, the fight against the Opioid crisis can be made more vigorous and effective. The root cause would be the needs of people to depend on strong drugs such as Opioids in order to function on a daily basis. If people were to realize the harm Opioids cause, they would be less likely to abuse these drugs. In this context, the prophylactic route is likely to be much more effective than to 'educate' an already drug-dependent victim, as the Opiods often alter various neurobiological pathways and make tapering off the drug very difficult. The crux of the long term solution lies in preventing a new-generation of Opioid addicts to form, a problem exacerbated by the fact that many babies born off addict mothers are addicts from birth itself.

According to the National Institute of Drug Abuse and CDC, the economic burden of Opioid abuse in the United States is 78.5 billion a year, a staggering figure that shows the amount of money spent on an abuse that could be allocated in another place. Also, 47,000 Americans lost their lives to this abuse of Opioid drugs. Opioids are a crisis that endangers people who have been prescribed medication and people with a tendency towards addiction alike, as Opioids are accessible to many. (CDC)

Progressive Web Apps can help assuage the damage that Opioids unleash on a community. For example, with diligent coding, one (a person or an organization) could code an app on the Progressive Web App principles. This app could show what happens to a person when they abuse Opioids, in probably a tad humorous but no-compromise approach. In a very insightful article written on Vox about the crisis, the experiment termed 'Rat Park' is mentioned. The experiment shows how rats that were socially isolated tended to use drugs in greater quantities and frequency, leading to these rats becoming very addicted to drugs in these environments. (Lopez) A suggestion for fixing the issues with these rats and in result people would be to create an application that addresses the issues people could be having with Opioids. This includes offering support on where and how to get treatment, keep a reminder on following up with the treatment course and such. In many developing countries it must be understood that conventional methods against drug addicts are very much lacking, and PWAs can help immensely here, especially for people who want to come off their drug dependence.

A prophylactic application and showing the progression that a person may experience when abusing Opioids. A humorous yet effective way to show people the dangers of Opioids would be to have a Heroin Abuse Simulator(Heroin is a pure form of raw opium), showing how the use of Opioids affects the function and daily life of the abuser.

A simple example of an app which can keep people interested and cognizant of the dangers of drug abuse would be a one which is to have a bobblehead on a Progressive Web App framework. Every time the person checks into the Web App, the bobblehead is increasingly addicted and affected by the Opioid drug. There could be a media aspect to this as well, so the user can share the progress of the bobblehead throughout the addiction process. Of course, the application should ideally have other uses (fetching news, some form of games for passing time etc) so it is installed in the first place and not deleted soon.

Another instance of how Progressive Web Apps can be an entertaining and striking to the audience would be an App Similar to the Oregon Trail game. The game could take place in a city instead of the Oregon Trail in the game. Similar to the former game, the character can start with a specific amount of resources and then these resources will slowly be depleted. Instead of food and water, the resources could be health, interest, energy, and mood. Then arrives the opioids, which put a further strain on the availability and existence of the resources. The player will soon realize that it is hard to survive with the use of Opioids. The moral choices the players can be egged on (at least at first) can be for the use of the drug at first, so that the harmful aspects can be highlighted. Real life examples of the end parts of the game can sum it up well. Some striking images of addicts before and after their addiction can be used, usually

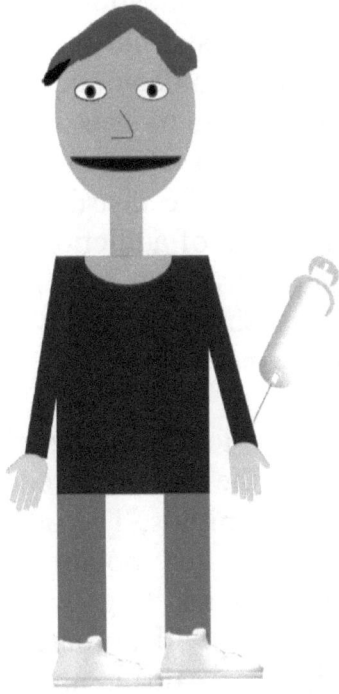

Illustration : A bobblehead showing the effects before the use of drugs. Simple illustrations are often very effective in conveying the message.

accompanied by putting a black bar near the eyes to preserve anonymity.

It might be argued that making a 3D game can be quite costly, even though the problem it tries to address, partially, is huge. However, with modern tools, a simple 3D game can be made in a few weeks with a very small team, and with the proper talent, a single person can also make it. Maintaining the application, however, will have some recurring costs, but they can be very low, especially if some outsourcing is done. Voluntary donation of sprites, models and scripts can also help in this context. Games and applications of this kind can also be distributed in schools and colleges, a hotbed of addiction initiation after the changes of puberty and peer-pressure. Inclusion of elements such as multiplayer play can make adoption very spectacular.

In conclusion, many people opine that half the problem of the Opioids is educating people of the dangers of Opioids. The other half is making Opioids harder to obtain and prescribing alternatives. Even so, drugs will always exist and even though they will be harder to obtain, they could be found in different forms. So, people being educated about the drug in the first place will stop the addiction before it happens. Computer application developers, often stereotyped as geekish and less inclined to consider matters of practical importance, can also get a refresh on their stereotypical resume, if their initiative brings a positive change on the statistics.

REFERENCES

1. Smartphones are a great equalizer.
2. https://www.researchgate.net/publication/2272 00039_Geographies_of_Global_Internet_Cens orship
3. World Health Organization, https://www.who.int/features/factfiles/malaria/ en/
4. CDC/NCHS, National Vital Statistics System, Mortality. CDC WONDER, Atlanta, GA: US Department of Health and Human Services, CDC; 2018. https://wonder.cdc.gov.
5. https://www.vox.com/science-and-health/2017/8/1/15746780/opioid-epidemic-end
6. https://www.drugabuse.gov/drugs-abuse/opioids/opioid-overdose-crisis#one

How Can Progressive Safety Apps Be User Friendly

More aspects of the safety apps that could be integrated would be tweaks to make it intuitive and easy to use. About the background, long story short, applications developed by many government-sponsored initiatives, especially in developing or newly industrialized countries, are often notoriously hostile in user friendliness. The reader of this book, if planning to develop apps themselves, must give their utmost priority to make the interface as user-friendly as possible. People must have a good user-experience in using the Progressive Web Apps.

While designing Progressive Web- Apps, the use case must always be kept in mind. It is often best to start with a blueprint. Should the Progressive Web App be made as hands off as possible? Should the user interface be made very simple?

The answer to the above question is an emphatic "Yes"! Firstly, as application developers, it must be understood that our perception of an app's interface is much simpler compared to a layman, as we are accustomed to working with complex concepts and interfaces. Secondly, when a person is under stress, it is difficult for them to dial or deal with a complicated interface. With a simple app, the person would be able to access help without being caught up in how to get help. Also, if the app has support in the background, the app will be more useful in the locations where help is needed. That way, if the app is closed, the app would continue to send the location and reasons for help, either to law enforcement or to other citizens. Privacy and related concerns are less relevant here, especially if the details of the individual are made anonymous by the apps at the first place.

Progressive Web Apps have the advantage of requiring only the browser-based dependencies to run. This means that device storage is not strained in order for the Progressive Web App to function. The link for the Progressive Web App can be put on the main screen of the mobile, especially for users not very accustomed to technology. This ensures for easy accessibility. In contrast, Native Apps need to be downloaded onto the internal storage and often require strict standards (such as a minimum API, specific frameworks etc). This is often unnecessary as the Progressive Web App may be the most useful by being used on the browser. Internal storage usage is not always needed for each app. Take mobile Facebook, for example. Typing m.facebook.com brings the searcher to the mobile version of Facebook. All of the features are not added on this website, but many of the vital features are provided on the mobile version of Facebook. While it is true that targeted ads are somewhat lost for Facebook, hundreds of megabytes are saved from the device storage. In this context it is useful to know that most entry level smartphones often have less than 10GB of internal storage.

As a detailed breakdown, if a user were to have a phone with 16 Gigabytes, the space left for other purposes would be low. Updates on the phone alone take up a gigabyte. Apps such as Instagram, Snapchat, What's App, Hulu, Google Maps, and Dropbox take up to 500 MB each. User chosen content like photos, Voice Memos, Music, Notes, and Email can take even more Gigabytes. In result, there are often storage issues for many people who purchase mobiles. Some gigabytes could be spared if the consumer chose to download a Progressive Web App. The functionality would be similar, but the storage needed would be much less for the Progressive Web App. On my mobile, the Google App takes up 250 MB. If a consumer chose to use the Progressive Web App, the storage could be curtailed.

An additional characteristic the Progressive Web Apps could have that would be beneficial to the goal of making the app good for safety, would be to have integrability to family and friends connection. This can be leveraged by using existing social networks as making one from scratch is often very costly to maintain. The cost-benefit analysis here dictates that privacy and related matters take a back-seat when wars and other emergencies are happening.

To develop Progressive Web Apps for situations like this, it is often best to research the location first hand and understand the needs of the people. Traveling certainly broadens the mind for a Progressive Web App developer working for Social Development.

In summary:

Some of the most useful advantages of Progressive Web Apps include:

- Easy updates and updates across all platforms
- Able to send distress signals over data networks
- Far-reaching mobile networks encouraging connection and capabilities in most parts of the world
- Usage through mobile browsers makes it easy for everyone to access Progressive Web Apps
- Does not take up a large amount of storage on the mobile
- Integration to social media allows authorities, family and friends access to location or distress calls.

HOW TO MAKE PROGRESSIVE WEB APPS: A Glimpse

This section gives a sneak peek on the way Progressive Web Apps can be developed. This section assumes very little background of the reader about the way software applications are developed. As with everything substantial, getting good at making Progressive Web Apps requires some dedication and practice. It is often not a tough problem at all, especially if the developer(that is you!) is interested!

It is important to understand that the Progressive Web App framework is a specific type of web application which can work offline. That is, Progressive Web Apps are a subset of web apps that, among many other things, work offline too. There are other ways of developing web applications that work offline that do not make use of all the specifics that are sometimes considered to be required for an application to be considered fully adherent to the Progressive Web App standards. With these things in mind, let us have a glimpse on how Progressive Web Apps are made. This is not a guide to make your own big app now, but a lowdown on the more commoner procedures and terminologies one is likely to encounter while developing a Progressive Web App.

Apps are coded using programming language. Some of the most common are Java, Python, C++, and Javascript. Progressive Web Apps are most often written in Javascript. Javascript is object oriented, meaning the language is focused on creating objects that store data in fields and goes through procedures also known as methods using code.

To begin, one must download programs to test code through plug-ins. A common Javascript Developer program is Eclipse JDST. On this program, a developer can produce and test programs and methods. The program is geared for web development and allows users to create projects under Javascript methods to the Eclipse Workbench. There are also additional plug-ins one can download to create Java projects.

The usage of Javascript is well known. Most webpages use Javascript in order to function. HTML and Javascript are the two main languages used to code websites. Together, websites can be coded, arranged, and compiled to cater to a developer's needs. The Progressive Web App can also be debugged, meaning removed of errors, and updated using the plug in to change the project.

Progressive Web Apps are supported by browsers, meaning they do not need a mobile specific language to function. To continue, iOS uses XCode and Android uses Java. One would have to code the program in two different languages in order to produce the app, unless he/she uses some other software tools.

Basic knowledge of HTML, Javascript, and CSS is needed in order to create Progressive Web Apps. Shortcuts and exceptions are always there, but for a beginner developer, it is very essential to know at least some of the fundamental web languages.

To begin, an App Shell is to be created. The App Shell is the aesthetics of the App. When one first opens the app, the background, menu, and heading are front and center. These are what one is met with when they open App. This needs to be programmed. User Interface and infrastructure are part of the App shell. As most users will interact exclusively with this part directly, the more polished it is, the better.

The App Shell is written mostly in HTML, as headers, font, text, style, color, and menu configuration may all be controlled with the HTML. If one were to make a basic Progressive App for an educative aspect, e.g. a safety guide, they would be able to have instructions and titles on the page. The app could tell the user to press a certain menu to ask for help. Another button could call family or friends for help, depending on the needs of the application.

In order for the User interface and infrastructure to communicate and function, the service worker caches (stores) the information locally so the page does not have to be loaded every time. Service workers take care of the offline experience such as notifications, background syncs, and history.

Additionally, the service workers are not part of the webpage. They run in the background through the browser.

Developers can make the service workers undergo the tasks that need to be run in addition to the App Shell. The service workers are written in Javascript and they may be used to handle requests and are terminated when not in use. The main uses are notifications and caching, and these can be used in a plethora of ways depending on the needs of the user and the context of the application.

To use a Service Worker, it first must be registered. This uses JavaScript. To run the Service Worker, the static assets must be cached. After running, the Service Worker will control all the pages that are under its scope. Development is done in the local host, while the service worker is used on the public page. It can handle fetch and message requests by the network.

Throughout the process of running the app, there will likely be errors. Errors in the Service Worker may cause the app to not request information or neglect to send notifications. In order to combat this, debugger statements and breakpoints may be used to debug the Worker. The Service often saves cache, so debugging this will allow developers to see what the Service Worker is saving when it does the tasks it is told to do. Debugging also allows the user to discern the way the Service Worker responds to different network conditions. HTTPS (A secure and now standard version of the HTTP protocol) is needed to run the Service Worker as it is on the network. If the user does not have a strong connection, the debugging can help discover how the app will respond to the weak connectivity. Similarly, if one user has a strong connection and another has weak connection, the developer can discover the rift in performance between the two users(although these are rather advanced methods). Some functions and methods may not work with a different level of connectivity. The developer can discover these when debugging the Service Worker. Cache is one aspect of the Service Worker that must be tested as it is a vital part of the functionability of Progressive Web Apps. Browsers have a limit on the amount of data the cache stores, so it is important to be wary how cache entries are purged.

When creating a Progressive Web App, it is vital to have Native Functionability. This will allow the App to be saved to the home screen as it is inefficient to type in the long URL every time the user wants to access the Progressive Web App. Also, it mimics the way Native Apps work, as the app is saved to the main page of the mobile. To begin, web app banners are a good way to show the user the availability of the Progressive Web Apps. Manifest is the tool that allows users to integrate the App to the main page on the mobile. Additional customization is also possible to do if the Manifest supports it. Colors, opening colors, and animations are possible with the tool.

The developer should be aware of the differing operating systems as some may not have all the features another might have. For example, cycling through apps on an iPhone is completed by pressing the home button twice. Samsung Galaxy app switch is done by pressing and holding the home button. Keeping the abilities of phones in mind, the app will be more useful.

A basic minimum specifications for a machine for a Progressive Web App developer is:
1. A system with at least 8 GB RAM
2. 64 bit Operating system, as 32 bit is getting more or less obsolete

3. Browser (Google Chrome is good for beginning app development)
4. Eclipse Che (On the website)
5. Web Server(There are plenty but Google Chrome has a powerful one: https://chrome.google.com/webstore/detail /web-server-for-chrome/ofhbbkphhbklhfoeikjpcbhemlocgi gb)
6. Given Sample Code
7. Mobile Device

How Coding is usually begun by developers:

1. Open the web server
2. Download the Bootstrap toolkit: https://getbootstrap.com/
3. Use the command here to make it a live server: $ npm install -g live-server
4. Start the server with:$ live-server
5. Go on the browser to
6. Access http://localhost:8080 should show the start page of the Bootstrap template
7. An app icon can be added so the app has a certain image on the home screen
8. http://www.favicon-generator.org is a website where one can acquire an image for the app image
9. Upload the profile.png file
10. Select icon for Web, Android, Microsoft, and iOS

11. The result comes as a Zip File that can be downloaded into the project directory
12. Unzip the archive to a new folder. We will refer to it as img/icon
13. Copy the HTML code that is given on the download site and paste that into the head section of the index.html
14. Adapt the value assigned to each href value of each <link> element
15. The resulting code should look like this:
16. Next, the manifest is used to have information of the web app and so the app can be installed to the home screen
17. This line in the HTML code that has been inserted in the previous step: <link rel="manifest" href="img/icons/manifest.json">
18. We may use that file as a base for the application manifest.
19. This is what the manifest looks like after the change:

```
{
```

```
"name": "App",
```

```
"icons": [

  {

    "src": "android-icon-36x36.png",

    "sizes": "36x36",

    "type": "image\/png",

    "density": "0.75"

  },

  {

    "src": "android-icon-48x48.png",

    "sizes": "48x48",
```

"type": "image\/png",

"density": "1.0"

},

{

"src": "android-icon-72x72.png",

"sizes": "72x72",

"type": "image\/png",

"density": "1.5"

},

{

```
"src": "android-icon-96x96.png",

"sizes": "96x96",

"type": "image\/png",

"density": "2.0"

},

{

"src": "android-icon-144x144.png",

"sizes": "144x144",

"type": "image\/png",

"density": "3.0"
```

```
},

{

    "src": "android-icon-192x192.png",

    "sizes": "192x192",

    "type": "image\/png",

    "density": "4.0"

}

]

}
```

20.   *Expanding the JSON content can look like this:*

```json
{

    "name": "My PWA Test",

    "short_name": "PWA Test",

    "lang": "en-US",

    "start_url": "/",

    "background_color": "#2C3E50",

    "theme_color": "#18BC9C",

    "display": "standalone",

    "icons": [

        ...
```

]

}

App manifests can possibly be generated from the beginning on this website: https://tomitm.github.io/appmanifest/

Note that the console.log is used here which simply print things to the console instead of the webpage. Therefore, this simple example just sets up things in the background instead of "going all action".

20. Add the Code for Website code in the index.HTML file. This is what the code looks like to be added after the <div>:

<script type="text/javascript">

if (navigator.serviceWorker.controller)

{

```
        console.log('[PWA Builder] active
service worker found, no need to register')


        } else {


        //Register the ServiceWorker


        navigator.serviceWorker.register('pwabuilder
-sw.js', {


        scope: './'


        }).then(function(reg) {


        console.log('Service worker has been
registered for scope:'+ reg.scope);


        });


        }
```

</script>

21. Access the website
http://www.pwabuilder.com/generator

22.The offline service worker is a good one to access because it allows you to use a local server to check how the service worker works.

23. Open the http://localhost:8080 and use Chrome Developer tools. Go to application tab and then open the manifest view.

24. See if pwabuilder-offline storage has been started and the first assets have been added.

25.https://developers.google.com/web/tools/lighthouse/ can be used to test the Progressive Web App.

SOME PROGRESSIVE WEB APPS DEVELOPED WITH A ZERO BUDGET

BACKGROUND

Making things move, in a developing or a newly industrialized country, is a phenomenally difficult job. Even if we keep aside the issue of corruption, which is unfortunately very rampant in almost any non-developed country, there are a lot of hurdles in making things work. This is one of the answers to the question we had when we were trying our hands in software development for the first time, back in the 90s.

"Why don't software developers have localizations (language and so on) for countries like India and many in Africa while they have them for small countries like Denmark in Europe"?

The answer is, of course, that software did not sell to any substantial extent in those countries back then. The overall GDP or GNP of those countries might have been large to huge, but individual consumers were very less in number and didn't affect the overall bottom line. Consumers had little to spend over their daily needs and more basic needs such as healthcare and education. This might sound harsh and a bit derogatory, but it is important to understand the context for the target demographics.

This also causes problem for any new initiatives using digital technology. Investors from government or corporations in developing countries are willing to take very few risks, especially for ventures that do not have the aim of quick market dominance and great profits through monopolization or other shady practices such as collusions. Governments also tend to put populist factors fast and are very skeptical of long-term strategies, unless backed by large organizations such as UN.

Amidst these looming threats however, there is a scope for exciting challenges. The proof is in the pudding for the targeted demographics. And this is to be done with limited funds available.

Fortunately, we were able to create some very usable prototypes of software applications aimed at social development. Quite a few of them have been presented in various conferences and got their humble share of acclaim. Mass-scale distribution of these software are being done, although some rough ends should be polished and refined for the maximal benefits.

These software were developed with a (virtually) zero budget!

THE GAME CHANGER- FOURTH GENERATION INTERNET

The rise of high-speed, high-reliability and affordable 4G connection during the last decade by cellular carriers such as Reliance Jio provided a very good background for these software application projects. Unlike computers, which in its present form, has failed to reach most of the urban households in this country, mobile phones(in its current iteration called smartphones) are found virtually everywhere. Due to the low prices of 4G, and the allure of the digital media, 4G handsets and connections are also found abundantly in almost every upper-lower class household and above.

Therefore, smartphones became a very viable and promising way for social development initiatives, as per our basic research.

In most villages we ran an informal pilot study, smartphones are found in abundance. More importantly, they are also used, both by the young teens and adults, throughout the day. Common activities included the usage of, just like a citizen of the developed country:

1. Web messaging platforms
2. Social Networking

3. Singing and short video making apps
4. Simple games, with one survival game rich in graphics
5. Applications for allied niche uses

The main difference was the lack of in app purchases or app purchases in general. This is to be expected, as having a smartphone is an affordable luxury for the target group and further purchases in software are extremely rare, if not completely absent. Therefore, any business initiatives can only be planned (unless it is a very lucky application or an effort by the largest corporations of the world) if immediate profits are less of the motive. Here this creates a partial vacuum which can be filled by small team of developers having an interest in philanthropy through social development initiatives.

The average time of engagement for different app genres were not tested as a part of the preliminary study but it became clear that many social development initiates can be organically incorporated into the lives of the target group with a low chance of failure. However, all individual applications should be optimized by hand to keep the users engaged.

APPLICATION:
MOSA-DOMON

A)Mosa-Domon : A software developed to educate the common man in developing countries about the threats of mosquito borne diseases and the ways to mitigate the threats.

Mosa-Domon, meaning "mosquito-suppression" is a progressive web app aimed at free distribution to the common man in mosquito afflicted areas. The main features of this app (still as a functional prototype) are:

1. Providing concise, scientific, and up-to-date information about common mosquito species endemic to a particular region.
2. Providing cutting-edge researched methods from universities to destroy the breeding grounds of mosquitoes. This also involves using compounds that are affordable even for the poorest of the users. The cost benefits also make it enticing for the government to adopt these techniques.

3. Providing methods for personal protection against mosquito bites. In addition to common knowledge, various new formulations are also discussed. For example, a formulation involving 2% Neem (*Azadirachta* sp) oil and 98% mustard oil (a common cooking oil) is also highlighted. These information are collected firsthand from university professors experienced and researching in this field.

4. Symptoms of mosquito borne diseases have also been included. These will be handy for users living in village areas and remote areas where these information are not popular. The diseases include malaria (kills over a million people worldwide each year) and dengue (specific treatment is very limited, usually only symptomatic treatment is done), among others. It is very important that prompt treatment is done on patients for improving their health-outcome chances and also to localize the endemic hotspots in case of an outbreak.

5. Means to contact experts for further information or emergencies are provided in the application itself. These will include

6. Last but not the least, for longevity and active use of the application, **a mini-game has been included.** This game simulates the swatting of a mosquito. The score is calculated on the number of mosquitoes killed in a set amount of time. This will also make the application appealing to youngsters and provide popularity when this application is distributed.

This application is created in its prototype form for many different target operating systems and devices. These include an Android version, a web version which can be played in the browser, and a version made for desktop computers. A progressive prototype version is also made which will make upgradability much easier and maintenance more hassle free.

USE-CASES

Mosa-Domon is made specifically for the common man of West Bengal, a state in India. Therefore, the language of choice is Bengali. Later on, versions in other different languages are also planned for different states of India and also for developing countries in Africa.

The main impetus that started this project is the recurring cases of dengue and chikenguniya (both viral diseases spread by mosquito bites) in the state which claimed a lot of lives over the last few decades. It becomes more problematic when sometimes the data is suppressed in fear of political backlashes. However, in the last few years, various governmental initiatives have taken place, which aims at educating the common man on how to protect themselves from these deadly vector-borne diseases.

Mosa-Domon can be used to contact authorities in case of a seasonal growth of the vectors in a particular location or municipality. The plethora of information about different mosquito species, straight from the research laboratories of universities, can provide help and allay fear against deadly diseases (as some mosquitoes bite only during specific times of the day). This can also create popularity for the government that puts this into effect (relevant because that is one primary criteria that the government considers while using a proposal).

To collect firsthand the mosquito-disease temporal data, or to cross check, Mosa-Domon can be added with new features. Data suppression by an agency for some twisted reasons can also be addressed by these means.

The main advantages of an individual application like Mosa-Domon are:

1. Clear about the purpose of the application. This is very important to popularize the application as compare d to a generic solution.

2. Possibility to distribute this application in schools (where smartphones are allowed). Alternatively, QR codes can be distributed which can be used when the student visits his home and shows it to a family member having a smartphone.
3. Possibility to distribute the application in various social development camps, and to allocate funds for the distribution of the same.
4. Independent data collection without sharing with the big multinational corporations. The big corporations are sometimes made up to be a big enemy but data privacy arguments are genuine.
5. Data storage can be made through encrypted communication to neutral servers, so that they cannot be tampered with. This feature is not implemented in the current version but will hopefully be done in the future.
6. Presence of noncommercial engagement factors (like inbuilt game as in Mosa-Domon) helps to keep the application installed in the device for long times.
7. Ease of debugging due to unified platform made possible through the tenets of PWA.
8. Ease of making new versions for multiple platforms, rich with updated data.
9. It is also possible to incorporate parts from other web-applications and websites.

SOME SCREENSHOTS

Figure 1: A screenshot depicting the main interface. The graphical polish is absent in these builds.

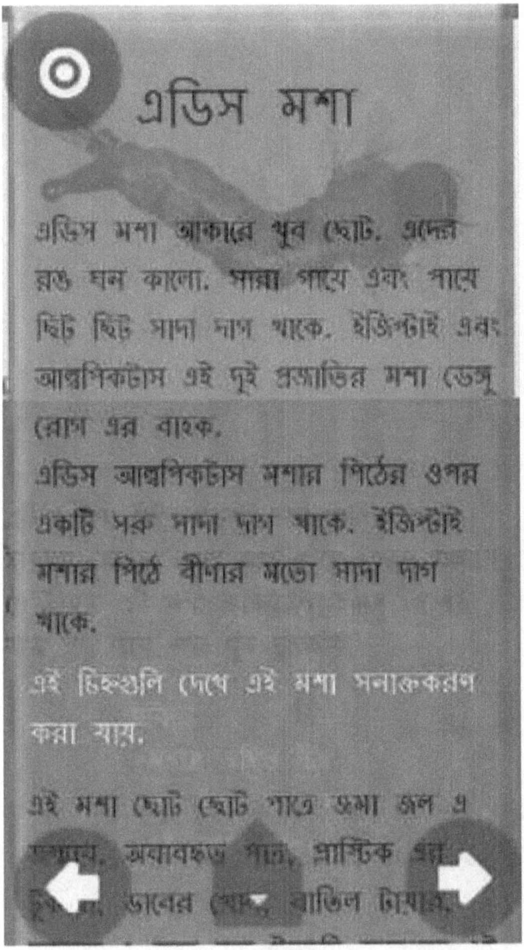

এডিস মশা

এডিস মশা আকারে খুব ছোট. এদের রঙ ঘন কালো. সারা গায়ে এবং পায়ে ছিট ছিট সাদা দাগ থাকে. ইজিপ্টাই এবং আলবপিকটাস এই দুই প্রজাতির মশা ডেঙ্গু রোগ এর বাহক.

এডিস আলবপিকটাস মশার পিঠের ওপর একটি সরু সাদা দাগ থাকে. ইজিপ্টাই মশার পিঠে বীণার মতো সাদা দাগ থাকে.

এই চিহ্নগুলি দেখে এই মশা সনাক্তকরণ করা যায়.

এই মশা ছোট ছোট পাত্রে জমা জল এ যেমন, অব্যবহৃত পাত্র, প্লাস্টিক এবং টিনের ডাবের খোসা, বাতিল টায়ার.

Figure 2 An overlapping plate showing the data about Aedes mosquitoes. Anopheles and Culex are also there. Included are the larval stages.

Figure 3 A screenshot from the included game. Here, the mosquitoes are swatted and the score is determined on the rate.

APPLICATION:
B-HEALTH

B)BHealth: Road-accident management

BHealth is a web-app with many different modules in context of public health. The existing modules (in late prototype stage) primarily aid in :

1. Promoting prevention of public health related problems.
2. Educating the common man about accident management.
3. Providing independent information about accident emergencies, including the nearest hospitals specializing in trauma care.
4. Displaying high-quality maps from providers such as Google and highlighting only the essentials relevant to the use case. This is important as most of the target group are not likely to be using such apps in the past and therefore lacking in familiarity.
5. In later versions, specific information with a temporal component about hospitals can also be included. This is very important for developing countries as the hospitals are usually not provided with adequate facilities for every type of accident (or otherwise) patients.
6. A specific component is aimed at providing mental health solutions.

India, the primary target region for this application, has some specific problems which provided the background for the creation of this application. They are discussed in the next section.

USE-CASES

India, the largest democracy in the world, recently got the status of a newly industrialized country. However, many problems still plague the country and the rising population pressures, inefficiencies of the government and low capital in social development initiatives exacerbates the said problems.

In the realm of health, specifically in accident management, there are some worrisome statistics that everyone interested in social development should be aware of.

Traffic accidents in India are a very major source of mortalities and injuries, which is the largest in the world. As per the National Crime Records Bureau, in 2015 alone, there were 464,674 accidents with 148,707 deaths related to traffic in India. These were formally reported and the actual numbers are much higher.

In a Cambridge university study entitled 'Prehospital Care for the Injured in Mumbai, India' states the lack of formal Emergency Medical Services in the most bustling city of the country. The average accident victim, to make the situation even dire, is a 'young man in late-twenties, from a lower socioeconomic class'. If prehospital (or hospital) care for the middle and upper class victims in the largest city of the country is lacking, what are the hopes for victims in lower socioeconomic class, in the small towns and highways throughout the country?

Many European countries have a law that states that it is illegal to abandon a victim of accident. This is slightly tangential to the application in its present form, but nevertheless very important. In countries such as India, road accident victims are routinely ignored by many vehicles. Common reasons include hassles by the police, instigative mobs who can kill and simple feelings of inconvenience. While the last one is difficult without conscientiousness from within, the previous two can be affected through change in the training of the police and laws and general traffic management. The refusal of hospitals to admit patients without relatives present, or other idiotic manifestation of policies also needs to be done away with.

Back to the use-cases of this application, apart from the laws and procedures themselves, the way to reduce the grim statistics is to make the common man more knowledgeable about pre-hospital accident management, and also about accidents in general.

As an exercise, the following question was put forward during a paper presentation in this topic:

"We see a road accident victim, thrown off his bike and lying at the side of the road.
Is in no danger of being hit again.
Bleeding is slight, but the person is unconscious.
What should be done?"

To make it simpler for the audience, there was a set of multiple choices as the probable answer:

Options:
1) Carry the victim as quickly as possible to the nearest health center.
2) Use a motorcycle if that is available first.
3) Just call an ambulance.

The reader can also try solving this question, although the local variables might differ from other countries which affect the answer.

The answer is actually none of the above. In certain circumstances one of the four might be an answer but in general they are not. This is because:

1. Carrying the victim to the nearest health-center as quickly as possible. This is generally wrong for two different reasons. One, the victim is in no danger of being hit again and is not profusely bleeding. However, there can be other injuries such as in the spine or in the limbs. Therefore, moving the patient carelessly (as probable from the words 'as quickly as possible') can be dangerous. Two, the victim needs scans like CT in an urgent basis which is not usually available at local health centers. The nearest health centre is usually much further away from the main roads where accidents usually take place. The journey to the nearest health centre needlessly lengthens the travel required, as the victim needs to be back on the road, on the way to specific trauma centers.

2. Use a motorcycle if that is available first. This is also improper as damages to the spine or neck can turn fatal in bumpy motorcycle rides. Ambulances and stretches are there for a reason. Motorcycles will generally be found first and the question doesn't assume that ambulances or other cars are not available.
3. Just calling an ambulance is better than the previous two options, but all the three options exclude a basic prehospital care which should be known to the common man. This is the reason why the answer is none of these three options.

The correct answer is to first check the ABCs (Airway, Breathing and Circulation (the last one is stabilized as per the question)) of the victim. Next, the victim should be well postured and then immobilized. Finally, a call to the ambulance for a visit to the trauma centre is to be arranged.

The posturing is very important. An unconscious victim of an accident should be placed on his/her sides, to ensure the tongue does not block the airway. With an airway blockage, a patient can very quickly die especially if head injuries are serious in conjunction.

Immobilization of the neck is another important point in basic prehospital management.

Information of these kinds are included in this module of the BHealth application. Additionally, the previously mentioned maps integration of trauma centers, way to contact the hospital authorities and related information are also included. As this application has a larger scope throughout the country of India and beyond, the language chosen is English, with the possibilities of including other languages at a later point.

SOME SCREENSHOT(S)

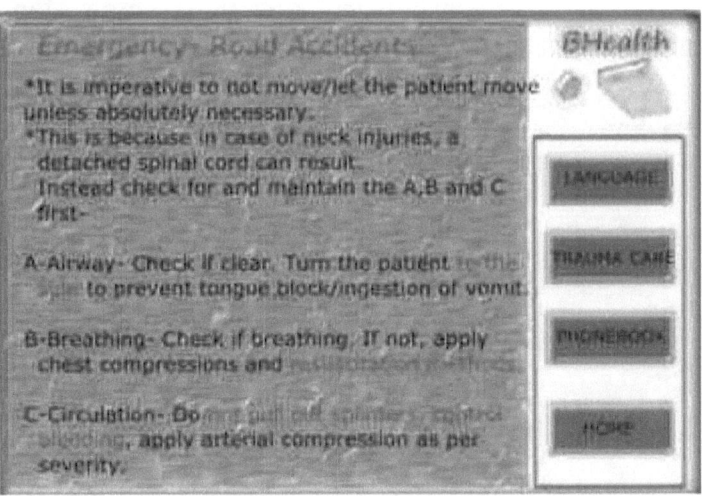

Figure 4: A screenshot from the early builds of the application. Here some simple textual information is provided.

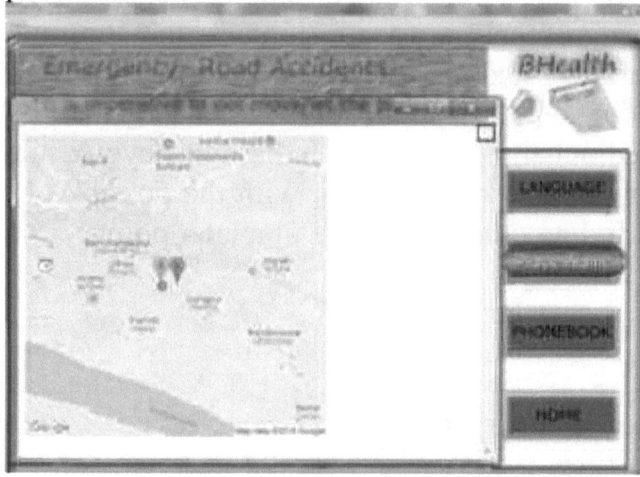

Figure 5: A screenshot depicting the Google Maps integration in the application. The information about specific trauma centers is also included, in this case, manually.

B)BHealth: Mental Health under the ambit of social development

It is aptly said that 'Health is wealth'. A right to proper health and healthcare is pivotal to the growth and sustenance of a nation. Fortunately, health of all the people in the world is being improved very admirably throughout the world by several international, national and local initiatives. However, there is one important aspect of health that is often overlooked or less considered. This is the aspect of mental health. In other words, it can be the overlooked aspect of a healthy mental fitness.

This application stays as a module in the BHealth app in its current iteration.

The application we developed, still in the prototype stage, primarily aid in :

1. Providing information related to general mental health and well-being.
2. Making it possible to take certain psychological tests which are the first line of screening, sometimes followed up by a visit to a licensed psychologist.
3. Providing support and information in gerontology based mental illnesses.
4. Providing contact information about psychologists in the area and also of health institutions specializing in affordable mental health solutions.
5. Providing morale boosting audio-visual aids, including motivational speeches (usually as website links).
6. It is planned that in future a 'social networking' aspect can be included with anonymity for group-discussions and being there during the times of mental-health needs. However, this is an expensive proposition and security and server maintenance can really increase the cost.

USE-CASES

Mental health is often less in the focus due to the many problems that hinder a simplified approach towards the solution. Firstly, mental illness is usually more expensive and harder to detect, requiring experienced psychologists and long sittings and tests. Secondly, mental illness often carries a stigma and that makes the patients fearful to approach formal curative methods. Thirdly, mental illnesses related to occupation/studies (workplace stress, mental harassment etc) are often swept under the carpet, especially in countries where the employees are more vulnerable.

In this age of information, however, we have access to many new technologies which can provide a promising way in the realm of mental health.

Many psychological tests can be self administered with the much needed privacy by the patients (probable patients might be a better word) and can greatly simply the next steps to take in the positive direction.

Other tests can be administered by professionals who need not be experts in the field of mental health. One such test, as an example, is the "General Practitioner Assessment of Cognition" screening test.

Countries like India, a good middle ground between developed and developing countries, struggles with a wealth of dire situations. Psychological counseling is very lacking in India. This is correlated with many variables, such as the suicide rate in this country, which increased from 7.9 to 10.4 per million between 1987 and 2007.

Another aspect of mental health which can be partially addressed by applications such as BHealth is in the context of gerontology. In India, from a paper entitled " "Ageing and mental health in a developing country: who cares?", the Result section highlights the following-

> *"Vignettes of depression and dementia were widely recognized. However, neither condition was thought to constitute a health condition"*

For a country that pays so much respect to its senior citizens, such an expression is nothing short of an abomination. Age related onset of dementia and related diseases such as Alzheimer's sometimes have no cure, but the quality of life can be much improved if the diseases are caught early and lifestyle changes are made to accommodate and in some cases, delay the progression of the diseases.

Crating awareness camps and manual testing by psychologists is a very expensive proposition for non developed countries. Sometimes they are borderline impossible, no matter the investment. This is because mental health deterioration due to old age is not confined to one specific geographical region but unfortunately, more or less universal.

Progressive web apps can aid in this context as they will be much easier to distribute, possibly advertised as a social development initiative in the radio (which many rural and some urban people still use in many countries) and television. The proliferation of smartphones in even the fairly remote villages means that family members (usually the younger generation) can administer certain tests for the senior members of the family. These tests must be of the preliminary-screening type, as definitive diagnosis requires expert help. Suspected individuals can take more tests or can be advised to visit relevant health centers.

With the growing promise of machine learning and artificial intelligence, the latter sometimes regarded as a subset of the former, the future hints of many exciting possibilities. Already we have findings that machine learning provides a better diagnosis of raw-data related to human pathological samples (specifically histological sample data). It is probably only some time until machine learning can provide insights into the mental health issues of senior people from parts of the map largely ignored by the mainstream media and not on the radar of profit-driven pharmaceutical business initiatives.

SOME
SCREENSHOT(S)

Figure 6: A screenshot from an example mental test included in the software application. This particular example is one rather obsolete test, but without permissions or agreement other tests cannot be included in the prototype stage.

THE FINAL WORDS

The wants and needs of individuals can be modeled in a simplified fashion by, among many other ways, the Maslow's hierarchy of needs. In his seminal work on the paper "A Theory of Human Motivation"(1943), Abraham Maslow used a pyramid-esque model and put the more basic needs of human at the bottom and the less basic ones at the top. This model also created a classification system where the universal needs of the society are at the bottom with the top blocks of the pyramid representing the acquired ones.

The bottom of the pyramid consists of psychological needs; food, air and water, to give a simple set of examples. Atop this stands the 'safety' needs, the need for a person to be in safe hands and not getting fearful or paranoid. Next comes the need of Love/Belonging, which includes the basic structures in a society, and the concept of trust. Then comes esteem. Finally, at the very tip of the pyramid, stays "Self-Actualization".

Unfortunately, the main forces that govern a modern society, such as the government and corporations, often fail to actualize these models. Sometimes, it is a lack of effort. At other times, the causative factors are greed, myopic visions and selfishness. The latter is more pronounced in governments which have fewer regulations by the public, especially those with a dictatorial taunt in them. Finally, sometimes these bodies try their best, and yet fail. In these cases, sometimes the cause is external factors which were not a part of the equation, random chances and sometimes the cause is purely idiopathic.

Social Development is a hard, continuous undertaking that requires cooperation and constant adjustments for novel situations. There is no magic bullet to develop a society overnight. However, the technologies of today can make things possible that were considered too good to be true just a few decades earlier. A country such as India, with its population exceeding 1.3 billion, has managed to put its status as a 'developing country' as a relic of the past. This is one big result out of the many hundreds of successful initiatives that have worked out and contributed to social development. Another successful initiative , with corporate roots, will be the effort of the Gates foundation, which has contributed billions of dollars for social development. The list goes on.

Progressive Web Apps, as touched upon in this book, can usher a revolution in Social Development due to its numerous advantages. The greatest one, perhaps, is its target demographics and reach. Many people, even those without a home, often have smartphones these days which can help them immensely to face the odds of life, if the right direction is provided. If we consider a slightly more developed version, or even the current one, of the application "Mosa-Domon", we can see how it can provide important information for mosquito eradication and emergencies. The tie up with local universities specializing in mosquito control also helps in this regard. Complementation in the absence of immediate profit-motives is also quite important in these contexts.

Accident awareness is another facet of Progressive Web Apps which can really help to save a lot of lives. It is sometimes difficult for people residing in develop countries to understand that how hard it is to get access to the emergency services elsewhere. In countries like India many people flee scenes of accidents and even sometimes refuse to attend to accident victims for fear of legal and police harassment. Accident reporting is very useful in these contexts through the use of one or many Progressive Web Apps. Specialized accident reporting and resolution, for example in the case of deadly snakebite, can also be done through Progressive Web Apps and it is region dependent. The author wants no future cases of "losing one's mother to a snakebite" to happen, as it happened to one of his college friends.

Lastly, in the contexts of the prototypes already developed, Mental Health is another aspect where Progressive Web Apps can show a lot of promise. Mental illnesses are often a subject of neglect by the caregivers, and it can be very debilitating for the sufferers and their immediate relatives. Some mental illnesses have no cure, but palliative treatment and adjusting the way of life can greatly affect the outcome. And many mental illnesses can be cured by using proper medications. In a country like India, where patients usually get a maximum of 1-2 minutes in an appointment with a government doctor, Progressive Web Apps can being a smile to the faces of an old father, a suffering mother, or a student too pressurized by studies. Much more research is to be done in this regard, both in the ambit of Progressive Web Apps and also in the aspects of Mental Health.

In the upcoming future, Progressive Web Apps addressing civil unrests (mainly in developing societies) and drug addictions should also be addressed to with a more focused approach. As both of these scenarios have a serious impact on the well-being of the society, and as a wealth of data is already available, these should be taken into considerations when planning a single, or a set of Progressive Web App(s).

With developers, doctors, caregivers and other stakeholders in one boat, and some persistence and warmth of our hearts, the authors believe that we can indeed bring a very positive change to the world with Progressive Web Apps. With the tools of the information age at our fingertips, the question is not now about "if", but about "how soon?"

www.ingramcontent.com/pod-product-compliance
Lightning Source LLC
Chambersburg PA
CBHW031254280526
45784CB00004B/1849